ADDICTION

The Way In.
The Way Out.

Simon Robinson

ADDICTION: THE WAY IN. THE WAY OUT.

This edition is a substantially revised and expanded work,
distinct in structure, content, and presentation from earlier editions
previously published under the same title.

Revised edition published 2026

ISBN (Paperback): 978-1-918532-03-6

Simon Robinson
www.drsimonrobinson.com

Printed and distributed by IngramSpark
Printed in Australia, UK and USA

READER NOTICE:

This book reflects personal experience and interpretation.
It is not medical advice and does not replace professional care.

If you are feeling unsafe, overwhelmed, or at risk of harming yourself, please seek immediate support from a healthcare professional or a trusted local crisis service.

This book does not ask you to move faster than you can.
Nothing here requires agreement, belief, or endurance.

If at any point the material feels like too much,
stopping is part of the work.

Chapter 1

I arrive already tired. Not newly tired—worn through. Time feels thin, as if I have missed something important without knowing what it was. I stand here unsure how I got here, only that I am late.

There was a long stretch where nothing seemed wrong. Days narrowed, quietly. I mistook the absence of pain for safety, and the silence for peace.

Something I was has gone missing. I feel the absence without knowing when it left. There is grief, but no body to bury.

I sense myself pulling back. I can't tell if I'm being pushed away or leaving first. Either way, distance grows, and I carry it as my own fault.

What once helped me endure begins to ask more of me than I can give. Relief arrives with conditions I didn't agree to, rewritten slowly, line by line.

At some point I stopped believing what I'd been told. Rules thinned. Promises felt borrowed. Even the story I told about myself stopped making sense.

I remember falling through broken steps. Others were above me, intact. I was already moving away before I realised I had let go.

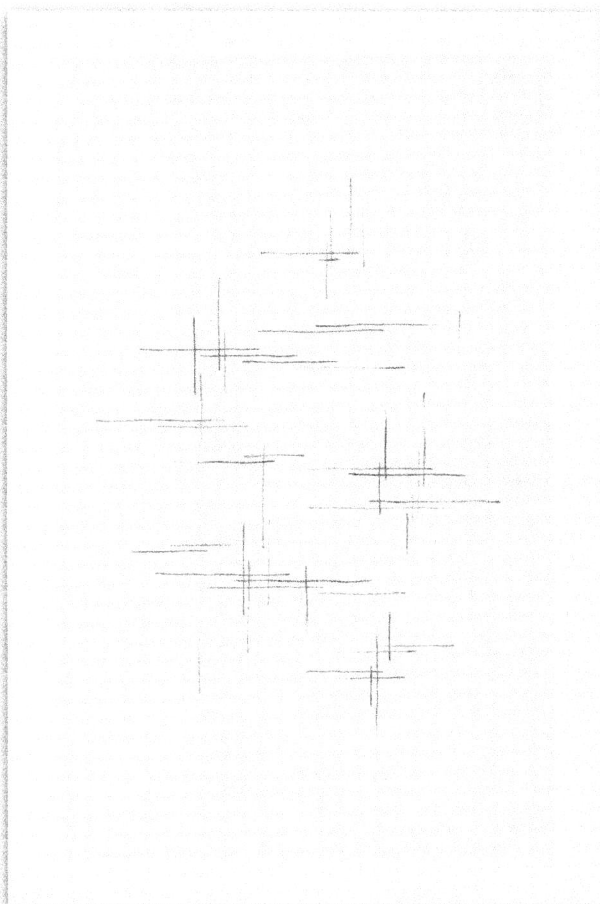

I no longer trust the world to meet me. I no longer trust myself to meet it either. The gap feels permanent, even when nothing is happening.

What I return to does not judge me. It asks nothing at first. That is its power, and later, its cost.

I am no longer chasing pleasure. I am only trying to ease what hurts. The measure of life becomes the gap between pain and its dulling.

I recognise myself in stories of beings who hunger without satisfaction. Wanting narrows, even as the hollow grows.

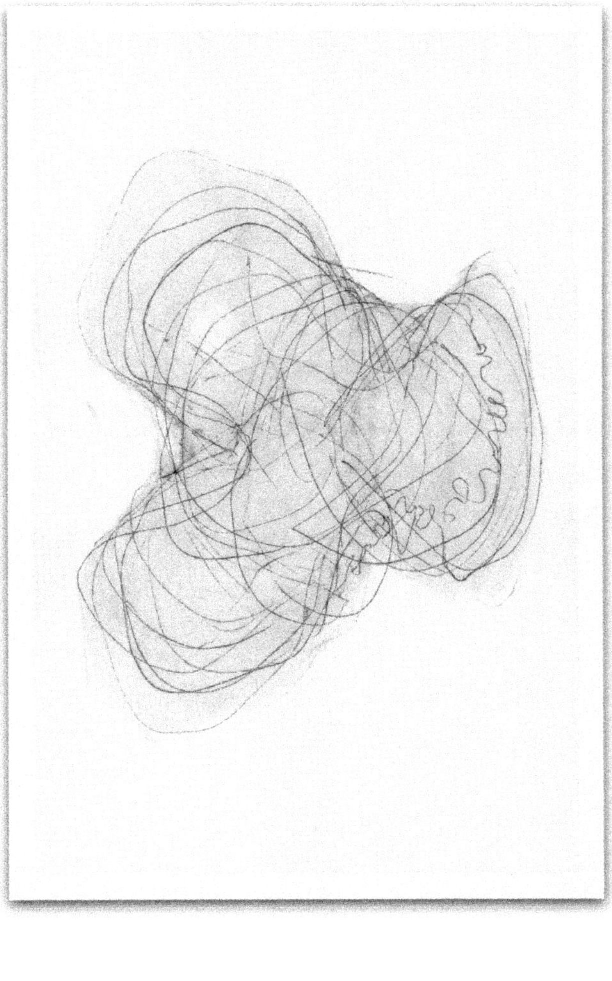

What I reach for retreats. I am surrounded, yet never held. Desire shapes the distance more than the objects themselves.

Everything collapses into two things: what hurts, and what dulls it. The world simplifies as it closes in.

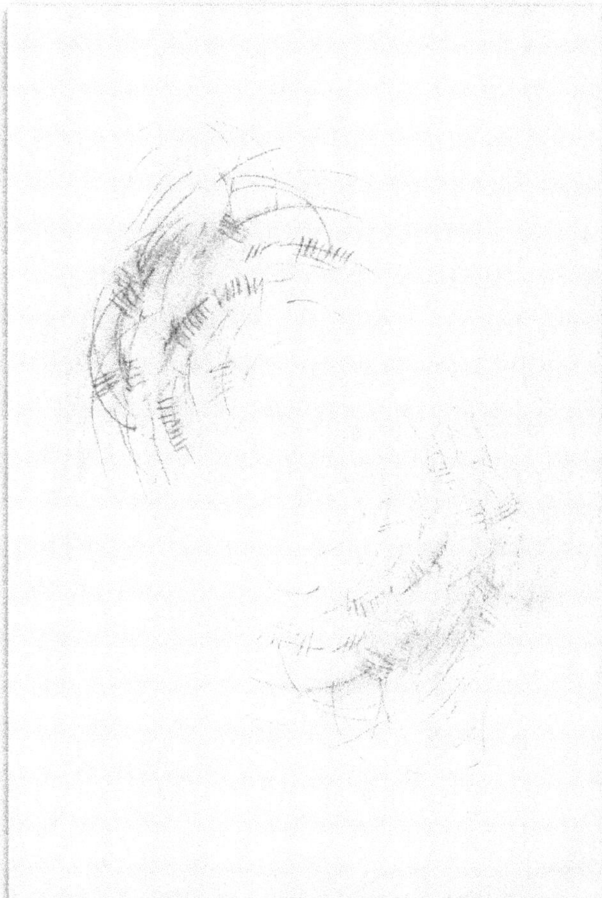

I am addressed, not rescued. There is no promise—only the sense that standing is possible, when I am ready to try.

Chapter 2

I carry the key in my pocket like a stone. The door is there, but I treat the lock as if it were a wall. If I open it, the room becomes mine. If I open it, I am the one who must decide what stays and what goes. So I wait for a wind that never comes, pretending I am locked in from the outside.

I look at what I reach for, and it tells me more than I want it to. The small habits speak first, before any explanation arrives.

I feel surrounded by invitations—quiet, constant, oddly personal. They arrive without names, as if already familiar with me.

I hide the thing I do. Then I hide the hiding. The second concealment feels heavier than the first.

The forbidden brightens. The "no" gathers warmth, and the edge begins to hum.

I can't find the bars, but my movements keep tracing them. The path repeats without distance.

Something hurts in a way that doesn't end. I circle it, disoriented, unsure where it begins.

For a moment I feel like myself again—lighter, able, smiling. It doesn't last, but it arrives.

I step out for a cigarette, not always because I'm right —sometimes because I can't bear the feeling inside the room.

I reach for sweetness when I feel wrong in my body,
then feel wrong again. The loop tightens quietly.

Even when I am "good," the hollow stays. Order doesn't fill it.

I see the same hunger everywhere—different outfits, the same need moving underneath.

Morning arrives and I'm still thirsty—sleep didn't reach the place that asks.

What I want feels like a return to something I can't quite remember. The memory has no address.

I'm spoken to as someone worth travelling with, even from here. No promise—just the tone of company.

Chapter 3

I don't feel inside things. I feel near them.

Like there's a clean centre where other people stand, and I've been placed outside the line without anyone needing to say it.

Even in familiar rooms, I'm slightly too far from the warmth.

It isn't only what happened, or what I did.

It feels older than that—like the self is the issue.

Not guilty, exactly. Wrong.

And the word sits there, heavy, as if it's always been waiting.

I remember fear arriving as sensation, not story.

A tightening. A flinch. A listening that didn't ask permission.

My body learned the rules before I knew there were rules.

The instinct is to run toward what should protect me.

And then, in the moment of reaching, I realise the protection has gaps.

The place I thought I could go—doesn't open the way I expected.

I learn quickly what is permitted to show.

Fear is treated like failure.

So I fold it inward, and I practise a neutral face until it becomes my first language.

My attention won't settle.

It keeps breaking away, scanning, checking—like something might happen if I stop.

Even when nothing is happening, my body behaves as if it's about to.

I hear words used about me.

They don't pass through; they stick.

After a while, I stop arguing with them in my head—
because arguing feels like more proof.

Sometimes something goes quiet.

Not peace—more like a shutting-down.

I'm still there, but far back, watching myself move and speak as if I'm not the one doing it.

I don't speak, because speaking feels like making it real.

And once it's real, it can be taken, used, repeated.

So I hold it in, and I become good at enduring my own mouth.

Some endings arrive before you have a name for what's ending.

After that, you notice who still seems untouched, and you feel separate from them.

Not special—just apart.

I try new strategies.

If I can't be safe, I try to be unreachably hard.

I polish a version of myself that doesn't flinch—while something softer stays hidden, unpaid attention accumulating in the dark.

A story comes back to me—not as doctrine, just as an image I recognise.

Eyes opening. Realising I'm visible.

The sudden urge to cover, to hide, to be back in the moment before I knew I could be seen.

There's a line in time.

Before, and after.

I can remember both sides, but I can't step back across it—not by wishing, not by pretending, not by being "good."

And even the troubling images—serpent, temptation, exile—feel like metaphors my mind uses to hold something wordless.

Not a verdict. Not a monster.

Just a way of saying: I lost my place, and I want it back, and I don't yet know how.

Chapter 4

I'm met like a friend.

Not rescued—just recognised.

As if someone expected I would return, and made space for me without asking me to be different first.

The previous material doesn't stay on the page.

It follows me into sleep, and returns as fragments—old rooms, old voices, unfinished scenes.

I wake with the sense that something has been stirred but not resolved.

My eyes take time to adjust.

I move carefully—not convinced the next step is safe, but taking it anyway.

Each small movement feels like a decision I can't fully justify.

A thought arrives that stings: some of my isolation is held from inside.

Not chosen like freedom—held like a habit.

The idea doesn't comfort me. It simply sits there, undeniable.

I hold an image of darkness pausing.

Not lifting, not resolving—just pausing long enough to notice a thin edge of return.

A dawn withheld, and then, barely, present.

I imagine being seen with too much clarity.

As if there were nowhere to put what I've concealed—
no shadow to step into, no angle to hide behind.

The thought is both frightening and oddly clean.

I picture a descent into a place that doesn't translate well into stories.

A private interior room where questions are asked and not repeated afterward.

Not punishment—just depth.

Not knowing appears as a kind of rest.

Strange. Unfamiliar. Almost forbidden.

And yet it feels like a place I can breathe without performing an answer.

There's a wound I keep circling.

I hide it, even from myself, and the hiding makes me hungry—restless, reaching, never finished.

The wound stays wrapped, but it still speaks.

I feel the urge to explain myself.

Then the fear follows: that explaining will make me lose people—bore them, burden them, expose too much.

So the words gather and dissolve before they leave.

I notice the bitter edge that compares.

It counts comfort like currency and pain like rank.

I don't like this in me, but I recognise it.

Something loosens when I stop treating my story as exceptional.

It hurts at first—like giving up a final protection.

Then, quietly, it becomes less heavy to carry.

I hold an image of taking hold—steadying myself.

Not conquering. Not winning.

Just making a quiet pact with what is real in me, even if it's difficult to face.

A thin crossing waits.

No rescue, no finale—only the sense that it can be crossed when I move.

The next step is still mine to take, and it doesn't need to be rushed.

Chapter 5

I arrive again, and I'm welcomed like someone who managed to survive the interval.

No questions first. No tests.

Just the sense that I'm still here, and that still counts for something.

Under everything is the same ache: the need to steer.

To stop the slide.

To make the next hour behave.

Everything points one way: toward relief.

The rest becomes optional, distant—like scenery seen from a moving car.

I notice how narrow my world can become without announcing itself.

I see how far I go when the next easing becomes the only rule.

Not because I want to be cruel or careless—because the need grows louder than the rest of me.

I watch myself obey it, even while I disapprove.

Even in comfort I can feel impoverished.

Time becomes something I measure and watch, as if the next moment holds the only medicine.

I can have plenty, and still feel empty-handed.

The bright interval gets shorter.

The hollow stretches out around it, wider each time, patient and familiar.

I begin to live in the gap more than in the lift.

I feel less like a person and more like motion.

Need moving through me.

A spiral that won't stop turning, even when nothing changes.

Each return tightens something in me.

Shame stacks on shame—quietly, efficiently—until it feels like weight I wear under my clothes.

I don't announce it. I carry it.

In the chaos there is still a repeating point—something I meet again and again.

Not an answer. A recurrence.

A small fact that doesn't move when the rest of me does.

I sense a quieter "I" gone silent while a louder self performs the day.

Not dead—just distant.

As if something in me is asleep while the rest keeps talking.

I grieve something I can't remember properly.

Like a dream that left only the ache behind.

I reach for the feeling of "before," and find only fog.

I begin to picture a presence coiled around what tempts me—close, patient, unreadable.

Not a monster. Not a saviour.

Just the sense that something is always there, near the edge of wanting.

Desire arrives like a lesson I didn't ask for.

Same material, different day.

I'm pushed to my limits in small, ordinary ways.

In the dark I glimpse a tiny torch.

Nothing dramatic—just enough to orient me for a moment.

Control doesn't look like force here. It looks like a small, steady light that doesn't argue.

It is easier to call my life weather. I watch the gusts and the lulls as if I were a spectator to my own choices. A casualty of the atmosphere. If I am only a ship broken by the sea, then I am not the captain who failed to steer. I stay in the wreckage because the wreckage is the only place that asks nothing of me.

Chapter 6

I take in the numbers and feel my stomach drop.

The road looks narrow, and the margins look thin.

It isn't drama—it's the plainness of risk, written down.

I feel fragile in a world that doesn't protect the fragile.

Not because anyone is hunting me—because life keeps moving, and I'm easy to knock.

The fear is quiet, but constant.

A sentence lands that I don't want to carry.

Not a prophecy—just the reminder that some roads are unforgiving.

It sits in my mind like a single bell strike that doesn't echo, but doesn't disappear either.

I rely on others, and then I bristle.

I want help and I hate needing it in the same breath.

The hand offered feels like care—and also like an edge
I might be pushed against.

The thing that harms me feels easier to be with than people who watch and measure.

It asks little at first. It doesn't flinch.

Human eyes feel sharp; the old relief feels soft.

I can feel the surface under me give slightly, even when I'm standing still.

The body registers danger before the mind agrees.

Every step feels like it should be simple—and isn't.

I sense a clever pressure that finds my weak spots without announcing itself.

It doesn't shout. It waits.

It feels like a test written in invisible ink, revealed only when I touch it.

A remembered scene: cold water, endurance, the moment of letting go.

Not theology—just an image my mind uses when it can't speak plainly.

Afterward there is silence, and the body feels older.

When I fall, a voice wants it to mean everything about me.

It tries to turn one event into a full identity.

I notice that voice arrive, and I don't let it speak for the whole room.

I meet the paradox: wanting out becomes another wanting.

The grip tightens around the very thing it tries to escape.

It feels like closing a fist on air and calling it control.

I move without a map.

And still, the weight of consequences follows my steps as if they are recorded somewhere.

I don't get to step "outside" the world while I'm trying to survive it.

I feel how easily need turns hungry.

How quickly people step away from hunger, even when they care.

Sometimes I lean too close, and I can feel the recoil before anyone says a word.

A tiny warmth returns, and I'm afraid my reaching will frighten it away.

I watch myself want to grab it, name it, secure it.

It feels like something alive that prefers gentleness to demand.

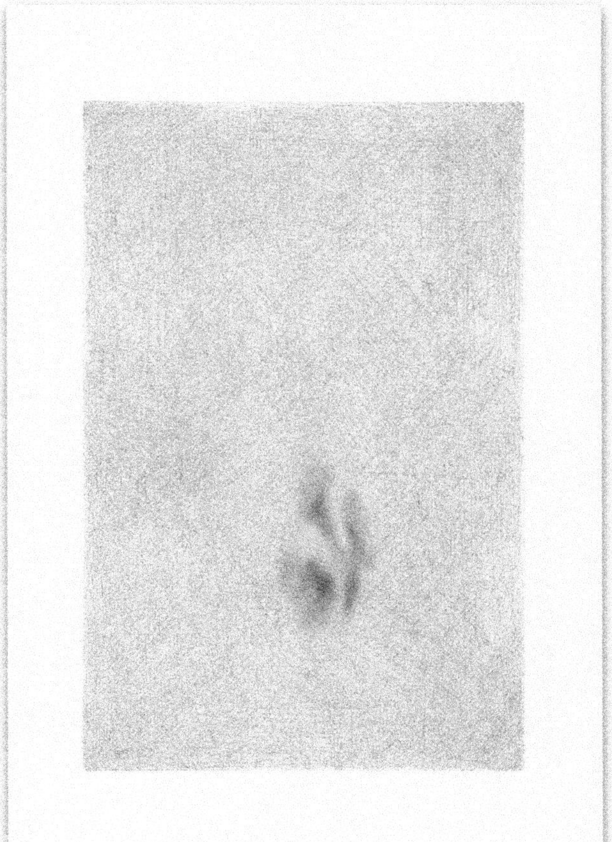

I hold an image of repetition—daily strain that renews itself.

And alongside it, a quieter image: the faint possibility of being unchained.

Not a promise. Just the idea that the link might crack, one day, without spectacle.

Chapter 7

I feel I began something long ago and never completed it.

Not a plan—more like a crossing I stepped into without being told what it was.

I'm still half inside it, moving as if the rules were always known, even when they weren't.

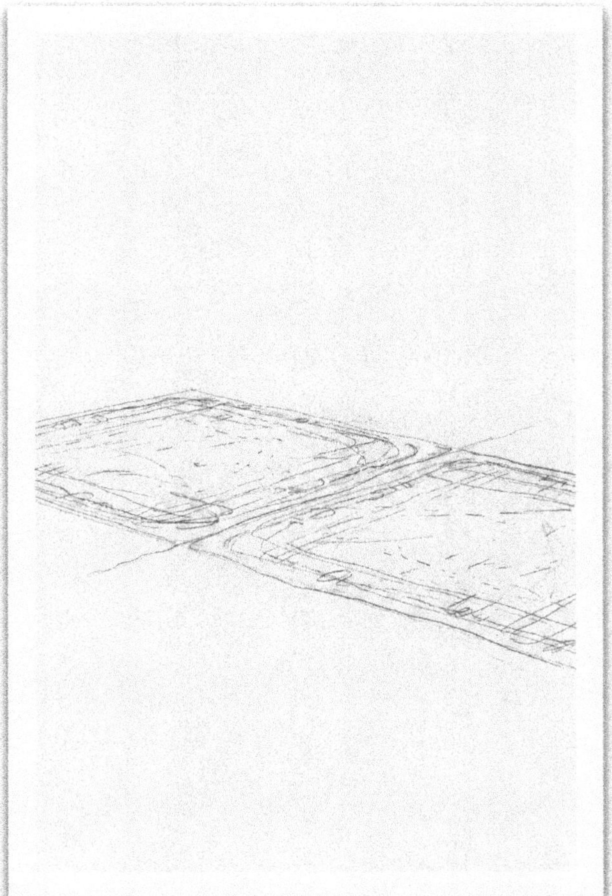

I recognise the feeling of wandering while awake but not fully present.

Days happen, and I move through them as if under a low ceiling.

It feels like drift with my eyes open.

I miss a version of life I can barely remember.

Like a scent I can't place—familiar, gone before it becomes clear.

The ache is real, even when the memory isn't.

When something bright enters, hunger rises fast.

Not joy exactly—more like the reflex to take, to hold,
to make it mine before it leaves.

Even goodness can feel like a trigger.

I sense a presence that knows my habits better than I do.

It waits at the edge of choice—quiet, patient, familiar.

Not a monster. Not a guide. Just a pressure that arrives on time.

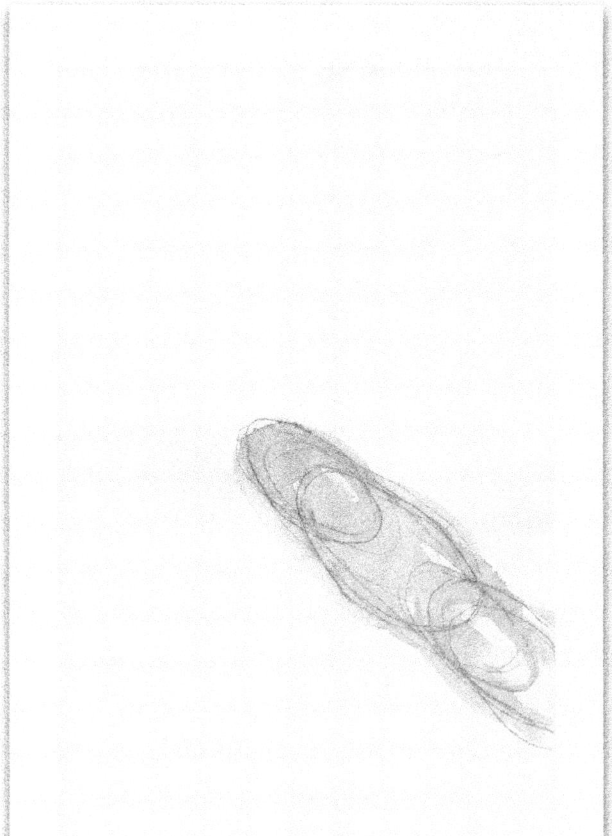

Part of me steps back and calls it a story, just to keep breathing inside it.

A way of saying: this is happening, but it isn't the whole of me.

The frame doesn't solve anything. It just gives me room.

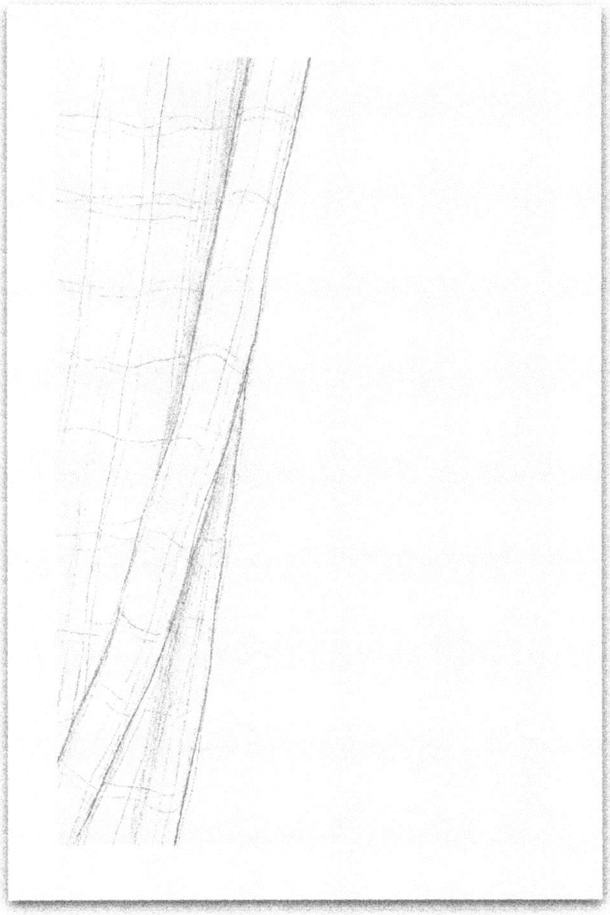

I feel the ache of waiting for guidance.

As if the delay itself is part of the torment—stretching time until it becomes a test.

I don't know whether help is late, or whether lateness is the lesson.

Then humour appears—unexpected, small.

I catch myself smiling at my own predictability.

For a moment the grip loosens, not because I win, but because I see.

I see how I'm fooled, and the old shame tries to rush in behind it.

It wants to turn the stumble into a sentence about who I am.

I feel that move begin, and I don't let it finish the story.

When something pleasant appears, I look twice.

As if it might be bait, as if sweetness must always ask for payment.

The suspicion isn't noble—it's just learned.

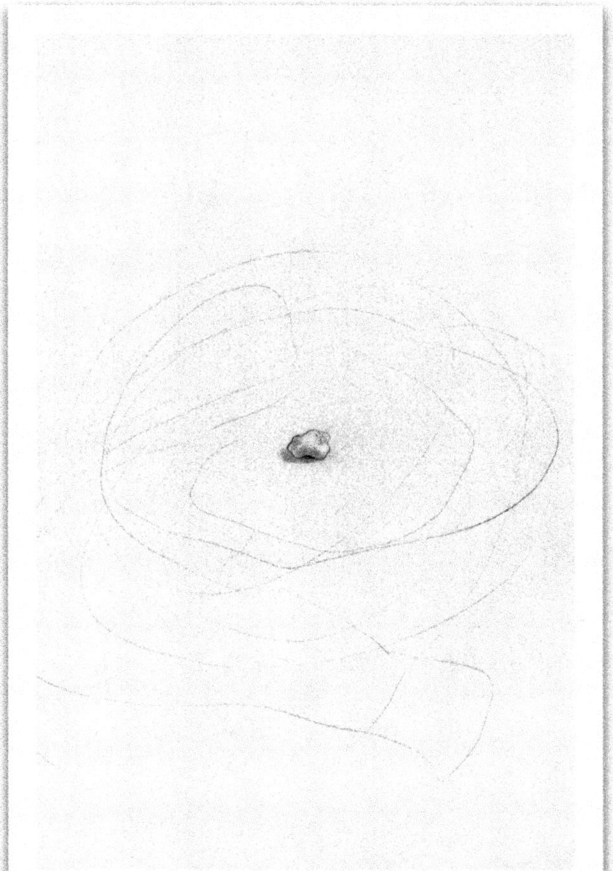

A repeated inner move appears: turning away from what reflects me.

Away from glitter, away from my own image, away from the bright argument of wanting.

Toward what doesn't answer back. Toward the unlit.

When I reach—even in thought—the light in me falters.

It's as if grasping is too hot, too loud.

The flame prefers a gentler kind of attention than desire knows how to give.

I begin to feel the choreography.

Something in step with me—tripping and teaching in the same motion.

I don't romanticise it. I just recognise the pattern of approach and retreat.

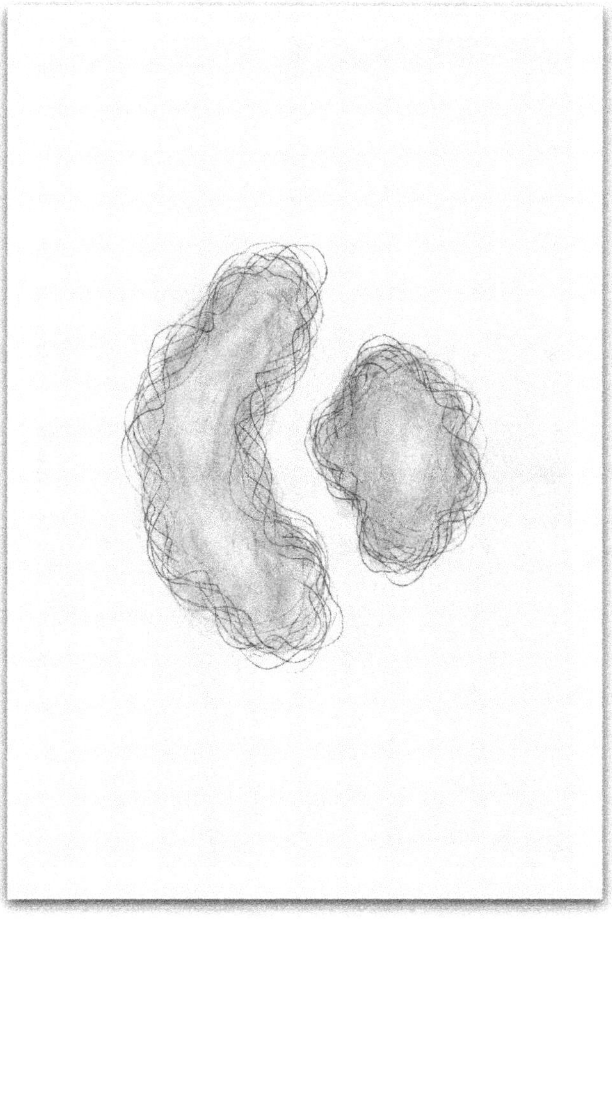

A new name approaches like a door opening into deeper night.

Strange, inevitable, not yet explained.

For now I'm left with the simple continuation: attention turning from glitter toward the unreflective dark—again, and again.

There is an adult standing in the doorway of my mind. I recognise the coat, the stride, the name. But I retreat into the smaller rooms, pulling the old habits over my head like a heavy blanket. I am not afraid of being hurt anymore. I am afraid of being capable. I am afraid of the moment I can no longer say: I didn't know.

Chapter 8

I picture what I tried not to see. Age. Sickness. Death.

They line up without drama, like facts waiting their turn.

Something in me drops, not because they are frightening, but because they are unavoidable.

I feel the pull of discipline, the neat promise of order.

I also feel how quickly it slips from my hands.

It isn't rebellion. It's gravity.

I hold the image of light being split from darkness.

I don't argue with it.

I feel the division running quietly through me.

My heart works without asking me.

It has been doing this all along, like a small star I never named.

I notice it late.

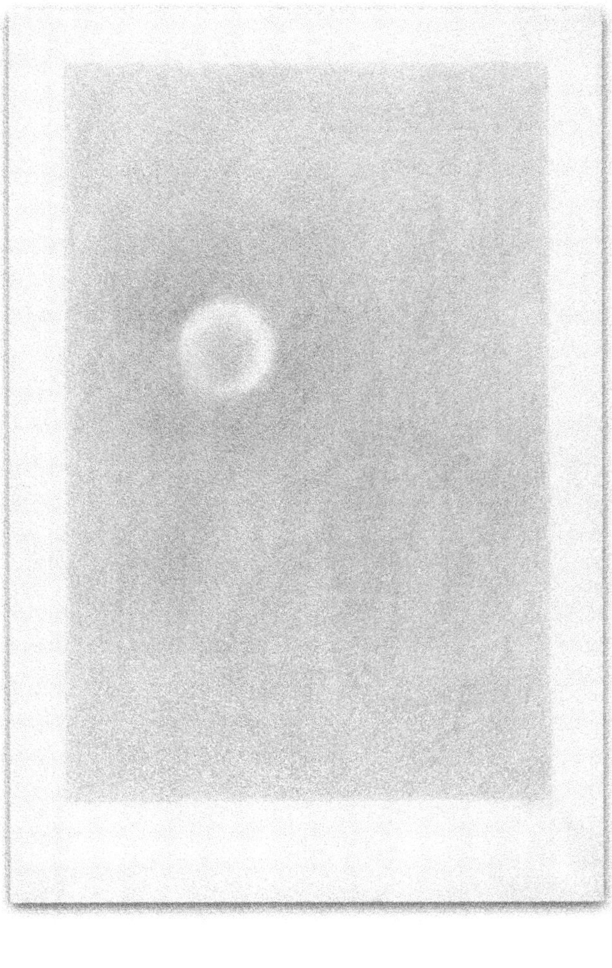

My mind asks for proof, again and again.

Names stack up, explanations multiply.

None of them feel like rest.

I recognise different versions of myself.

One sleeps. One searches. One stays just out of reach.

I don't arrange them. I just see them.

Some parts of me feel light.

The heavier parts arrive earlier and linger longer.

They know the way back.

I imagine something of me drifting on.

Not freed. Not transformed.

Still carrying my patterns, looking for somewhere to land.

A defence falls away.

I can't tell myself I'm fine anymore.

There is no performance left in this moment.

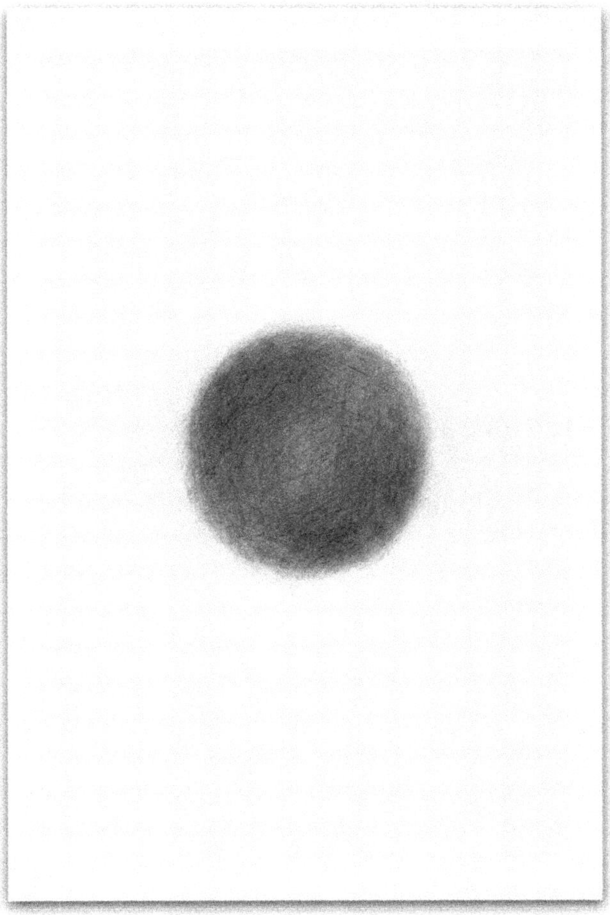

Doubt presses like weather in my chest.

It doesn't ask questions.

It just stays.

Part of me wants a simple fix.

Another part knows the trouble isn't located in one place.

They don't argue. They coexist.

I feel separated into pieces.

Names, roles, histories loosen their grip.

None of them hold on their own.

I don't know where to go.

The admission is bleak.

It is also clean.

I'm tired from carrying it all at once.

I let the day end without finishing the thought.

Tomorrow can wait.

Chapter 9

I'm struck by how little of me feels singular.

Breath arrives. Blood moves. Digestion turns.

Signals fire, decisions tilt, before I can claim them.

It isn't sinister. It's just strange.

As if "I" is late to the meeting—always.

I remember moments when my body moved first.

A word spoken before I meant it.

A hand reaching, already committed, while my mind scrambled to catch up.

Afterwards, I replayed it as if the replay could rewrite it.

But the sequence stayed the same: motion, then story.

Most of what keeps me alive happens in silence.

The quiet isn't proof of peace—it's a kind of cover.

A smooth lid over a churning apparatus.

Sometimes I sense the pressure underneath and realise:

my calmness can be manufactured, and my panic can be too.

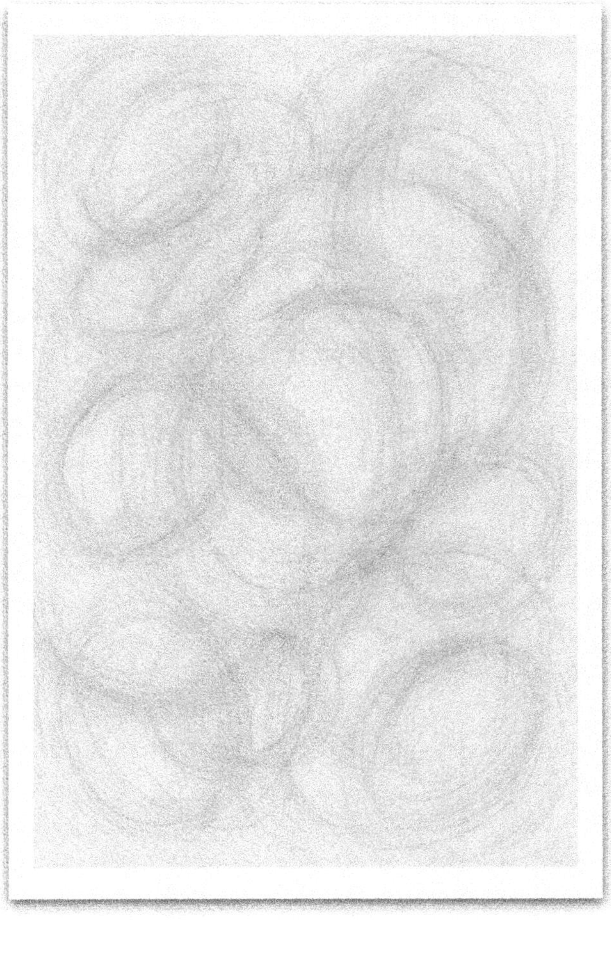

A feeling tightens and I can't name it.

It behaves like a warning, even when nothing is happening.

My mind leans toward it, as if attention could solve it,

and the leaning becomes its own ache.

It's pain without a clear wound.

When there's less to do, my thoughts get louder.

The room doesn't change, but the atmosphere does.

I circle the same questions until they feel like walls.

It isn't insight. It's exposure—too much mind in too little space.

I can feel how awareness might have started:

a small animal-watchfulness, scanning for threat.

Control as a reflex, not a virtue.

A tightening around the idea that survival depends on grip.

Even now, that old posture wakes easily.

Shame isn't always a sentence in my head.

Sometimes it's a distance.

A slight misalignment between me and everything else,

as if I'm a half-step out of register with the world.

I don't even know what I'm answering for—only that I'm answering.

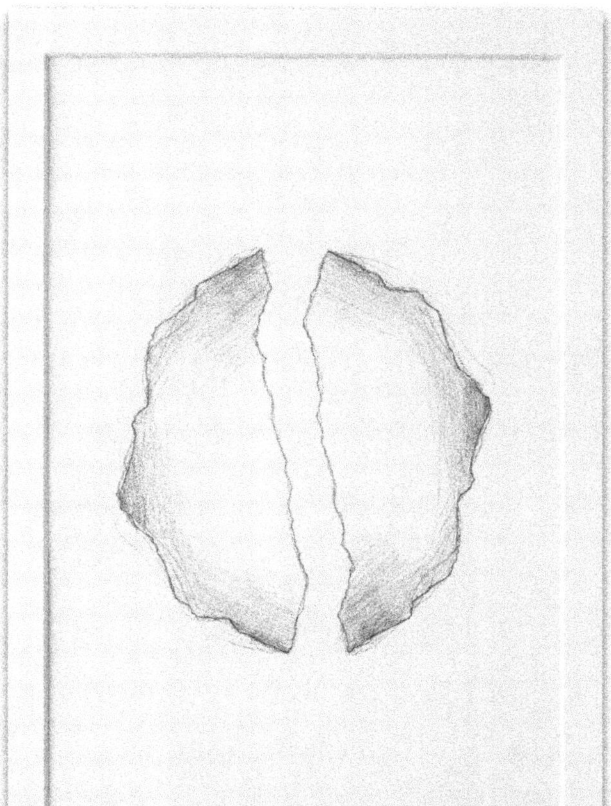

Wanting doesn't stay in its lane.

It spreads—past hunger, past need—

and starts attaching itself to anything that looks like relief.

Not because the thing is beautiful,

but because the ache is loud.

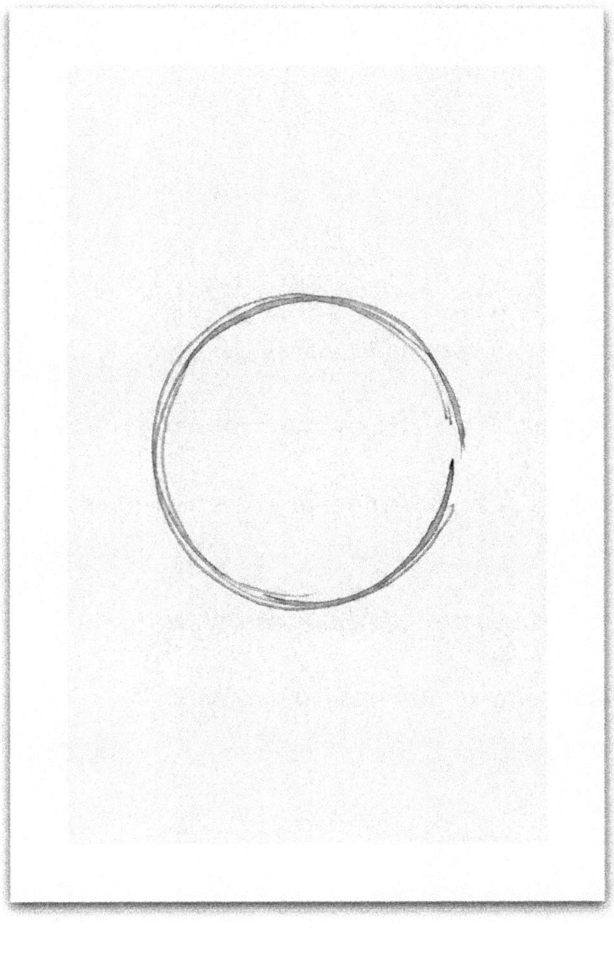

There's something quieter than thought.

It doesn't argue. It doesn't perform.

When I'm busy lying—to others or to myself—it recedes,

not as punishment, just as consequence.

And I notice the dimming only later.

Extremes call to each other.

If I tighten, something in me rebels.

If I loosen, something in me panics.

It becomes a private weather system:

gusts, lulls, and no stable forecast.

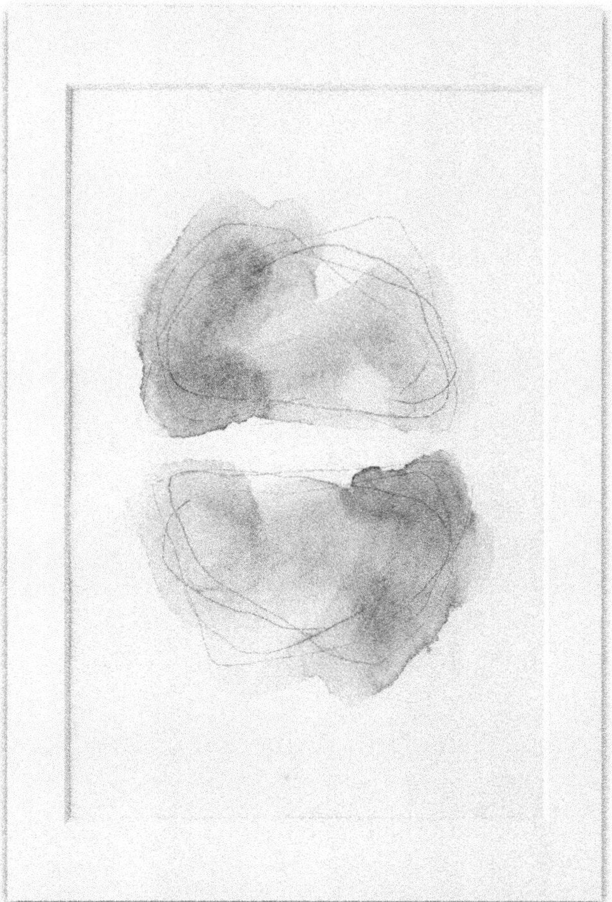

I recognise the scattered feeling again.

Not dramatic—just dispersed.

As if the "me" I rely on is made of pieces...

and someone has set them down in different rooms.

I keep walking between them, trying to gather myself quietly.

There are moments when everything feels visible at the same time—

processes, motives, reactions, histories—layered and moving.

It isn't triumph.

It's too bright in the mind, like standing too close to a plain white wall in midday.

I wobble under the amount.

Awe can tip into fear.

Not because the world is wrong—

but because my capacity is finite.

I feel myself pull back, not as failure,

as a kind of mercy.

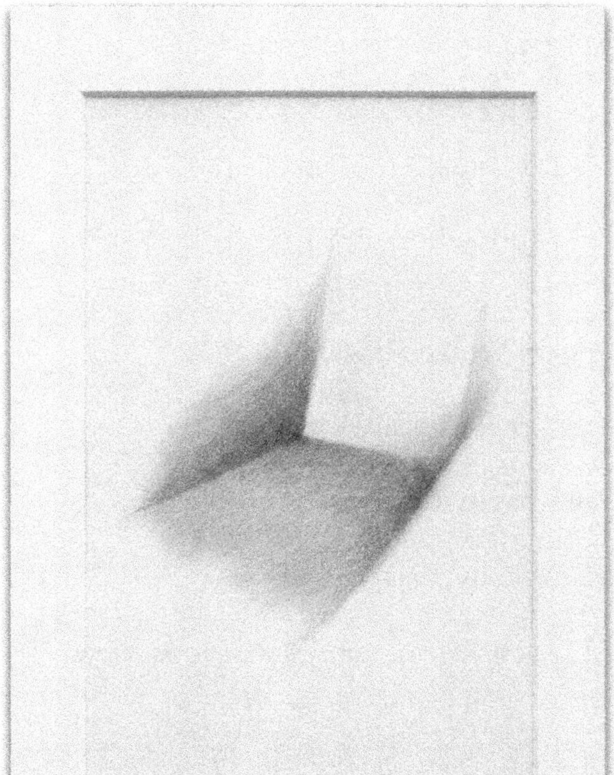

I'm spent from carrying it all at once.

The day ends without a conclusion.

I don't convert what happened into a lesson.

I let it settle as weight and wonder,

and I give myself the simplest thing: tomorrow.

Chapter 10

I'm met gently, not as a solution, but as a presence.

Like someone checking in after a long walk, noticing my pace.

The body I'm in feels older than the hour.

I don't explain myself. I just stand there and let the moment be shared.

The bells announce the hour whether I'm ready or not.

They don't ask how I'm doing.

They don't soften for my mood.

They simply ring, and the day reshapes itself around the sound.

Words can lift me.

Words can trap me.

Sometimes the same phrase does both—

a handle and a hook in one small sound.

I feel how language shapes the inside of my chest.

I imagine turning toward something too bright to hold.

Not holiness—just intensity.

The body goes flat, as if the system has overloaded.

Afterwards there's no explanation, only the memory of being outmatched.

Everything returns.

The same impulses, the same bargains, the same tired aftermath.

I don't choose the circle so much as notice I'm already in it.

Even resistance can become part of the rotation.

Ageing. Sickness. Death.

They appear again as plain facts, not threats.

I can't negotiate with them, and I can't outrun them.

The shock isn't that they exist—

it's that I kept living as if they didn't.

I feel the risk of reaching for what I can't prove.

Not because it's noble—

because everything else has failed to carry the weight.

My foot hovers over a darkness that might be nothing at all.

When faith thins, odd things start to seem possible.

Not because I believe—

because I'm tired of the usual routes.

Even an impossible quest can look like a doorway when the room is burning down inside me.

The sun sets again.

It does this without consulting my state of mind.

It will rise again whether I do or not.

I watch the edge of light go and feel how ordinary endings are.

I picture a slow journey through darkness.

Not punishment—movement.

Gates closing behind me, one after another, not slamming—just shutting.

The mind keeps count. The body keeps walking.

I feel parts of myself being measured.

Not by a god—by consequence, by memory, by the way things add up.

Some days the scales tilt before I speak.

I stand there and feel the unevenness.

Old splits still ache.

Not as stories, but as sensations—

a flinch, a tightness, a sudden blankness where something should be.

Time passes, and the seam remains.

Something feels unmoving.

Not a truth—just a sense of steadiness I can't hold for long.

I spin around it: moods, cravings, shame, relief.

The centre doesn't rescue me. It simply doesn't move.

Night falls without a lesson.

I don't make a meaning out of it.

I feel the day's weight, and I let it settle.

Rest isn't victory. It's the only honest next step I have.

Chapter 11

Morning meets me like a companion.

The air feels clean, almost forgiving.

And still—something in me stays braced, as if the day has an old appointment I can't cancel.

I walk into the light without calling it safety.

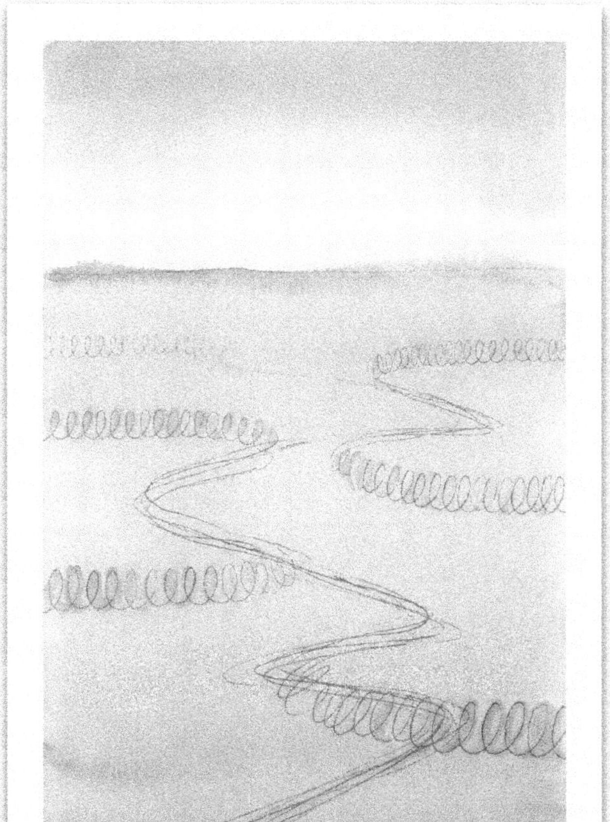

I hear the old names for the same shape.

Different tongues, different stories, one familiar curve.

I don't need to believe the myths to recognise the pattern.

It arrives in me like a remembered sound.

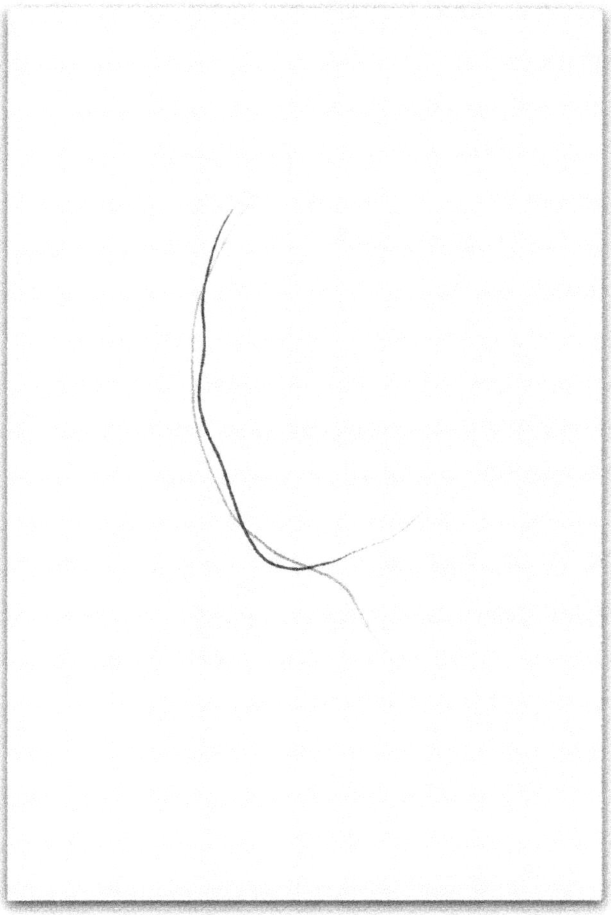

It isn't distant.

It lives close to my choices—close to my mouth, close to my hands.

It doesn't roar. It waits.

And the waiting is part of the pressure.

I feel myself held at the edge.

Wanting to belong. Refusing the terms of belonging.

Not because I'm brave—because I'm tired of pretending.

The distance isn't geography. It's a posture I can't fully put down.

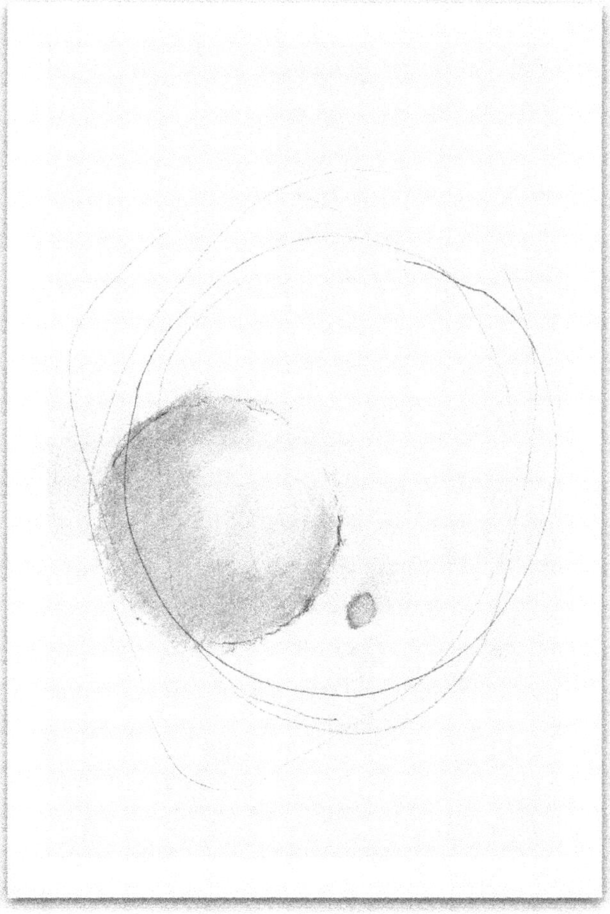

I picture a box that fits too well.

Smooth edges. Clean lid.

It looks safe from the outside.

Inside, there's no air for anything human.

I sense my life as pieces.

Names. Roles. Urges. Old scenes that still pull at me.

They don't assemble on command.

And there's always one thing missing that I can't name without inventing it.

I hold the image of something wrapped with care.

Not celebrated. Not solved.

Simply tended to, as if tenderness could exist without a reason.

The gesture feels older than my arguments.

I remember an unbroken kind of being.

Before I sorted myself into good and bad.

I can't return to it by effort.

But sometimes I feel its outline, like a shoreline seen through mist.

There's a realm in me where need is louder than words.

Grief becomes motion, not meaning.

Reaching happens before asking.

And the reach never lands where it thinks it will.

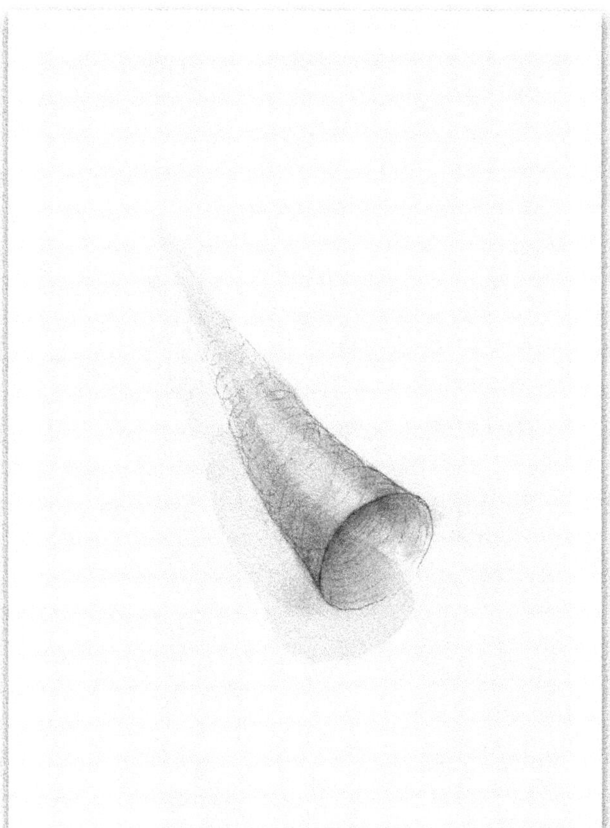

The pattern returns with the day.

Strain, relapse, repair—just enough to begin again.

It doesn't feel like punishment.

It feels like a mechanism that keeps turning whether I agree or not.

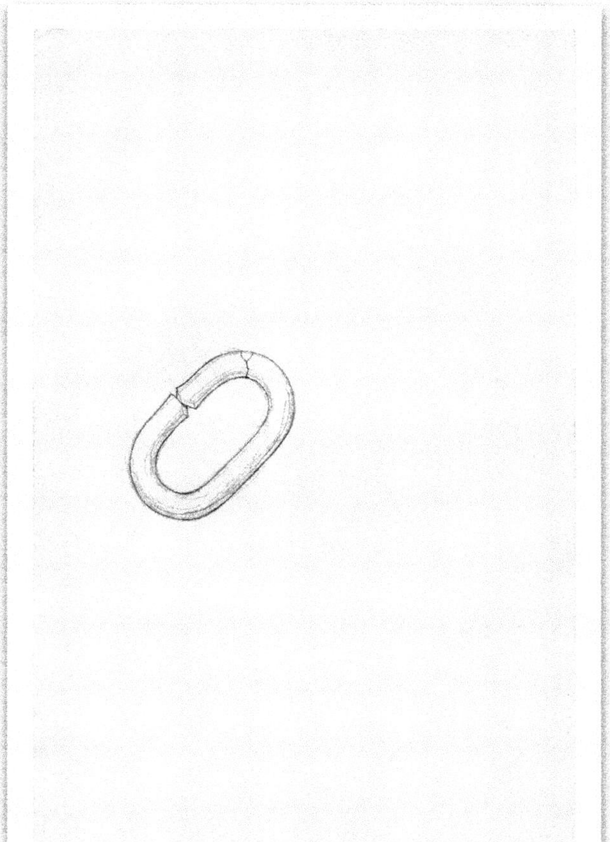

In the night I imagine my heart on scales.

Not in a courtroom—just in the dark, where the mind measures itself.

I wake as if the verdict were physical.

Heavy or light, before I've done anything at all.

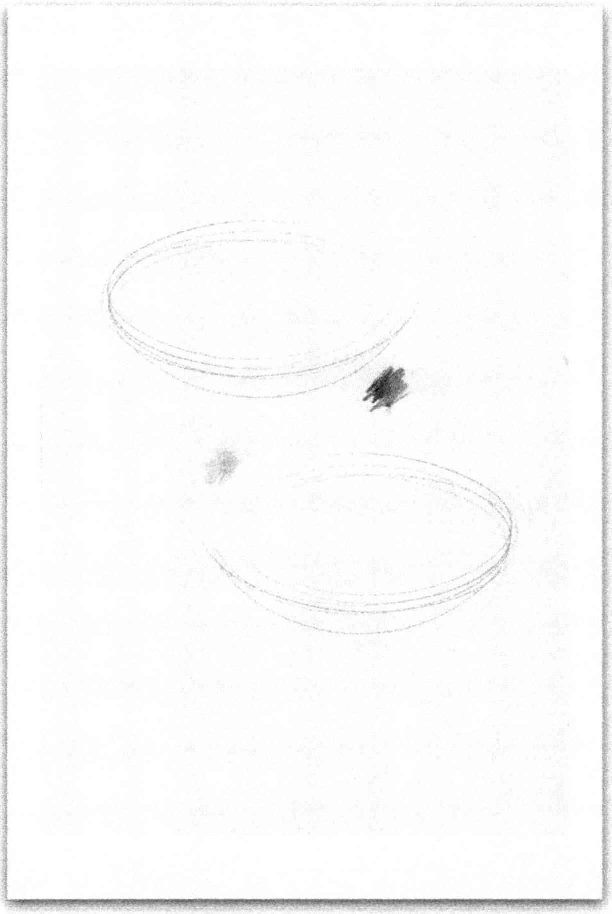

As I fall asleep, the world turns down like a dial.

Edges soften. Names lose their grip.

I become unfamiliar to myself, quietly, without drama.

Not gone—just shifted into another mode.

I remember waking clean once.

Light, ordinary, unhaunted.

Not ecstatic—just present.

Like sunrise inside the ribs, small and believable.

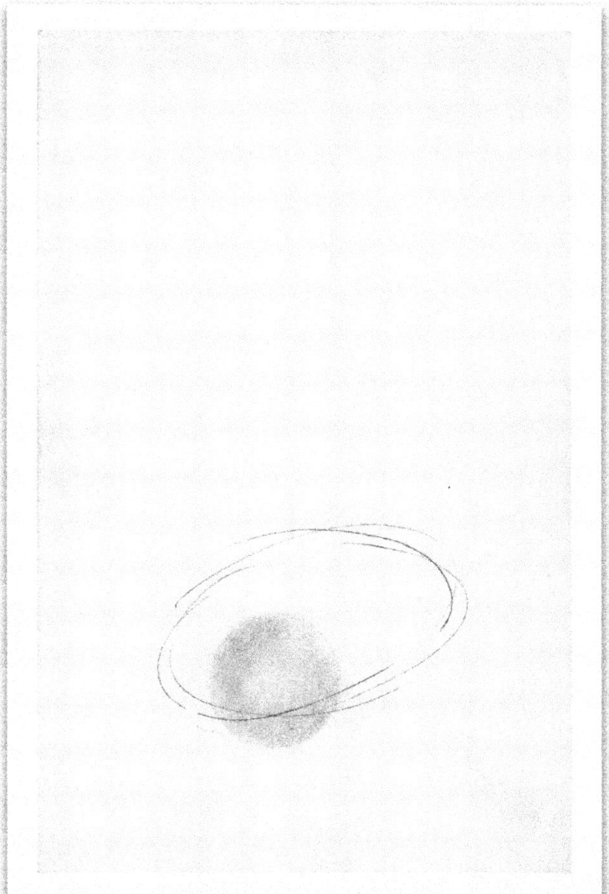

Other mornings I wake hollow.

The thing that used to soothe me doesn't land the same when I'm watching myself.

Shame doesn't shout—it observes.

And the observation changes the taste of relief.

I don't claim a victory.

I feel the day settle into the body like food after hunger —heavy, real, unfinished.

The cycle remains.

I rest inside that fact, not as surrender, as pacing.

And I let the next turning come when it comes.

I watch my hands move and I disown the motion. A hand reaching. A hand taking. A hand covering. I treat them like strangers I am forced to live with. Because if they are mine, then the reach is mine. And if the reach is mine, I must decide where it stops. And I am not yet ready to be the one who says: No.

Chapter 12

I remember how often the body mends in its own time.

A cut closes. A bruise fades. A fever breaks.

I feel quiet awe at that patience.

I also feel a quiet impatience, as if I want the timetable in advance.

I feel the hunger under everything.

Less for pleasure than for return—

for a brief before the before,

when I didn't need to negotiate with myself to feel okay.

Part of me settles into the story of being harmed.

Another part keeps scanning for a pattern, like a detective with no case file.

I move between them without choosing.

The swing itself becomes the atmosphere.

Some days I'm hollow and restless.

Other days I'm full of heat, pushing and pulling at everything.

Neither state feels like truth.

Both feel like weather moving through a house.

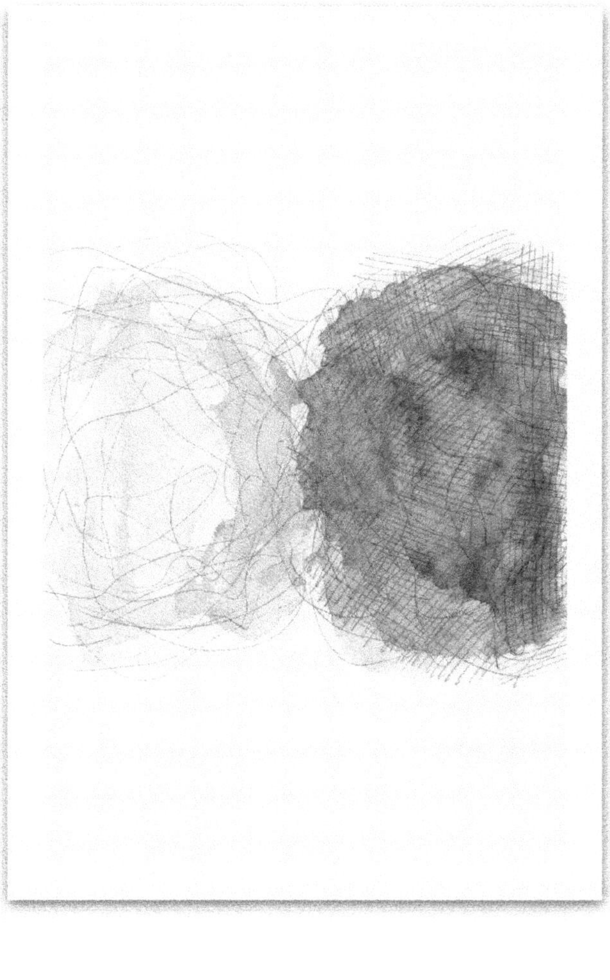

I notice how much of me has gone missing.

I keep reaching for a person I used to be.

The reach closes on air.

The grief is real, even when I can't name what it's for.

When I look inward, I can't tell who is looking.

I can't tell who is being looked at.

The split makes me dizzy—

not mystical, just disorienting, like standing too close to a mirror.

A harsh voice measures me.

I try to measure the voice back, and it slips away.

It leaves me holding the verdict with no court,

as if the sentence wrote itself.

I recognise different versions of myself.

One drifts. One searches. One is briefly clear.

None of them stays long enough to become a home.

I watch the shifts and feel how temporary "me" can be.

Doubt arrives like a pain that won't locate itself.

I feel lonelier, and also less certain of my mask.

Something I used to call "confidence" thins out.

What remains is quieter, and harder to perform.

I sense two currents in me pulling against each other —feeling and thought—neither willing to yield.

The strain isn't philosophical.

It's bodily: a tightness, a tremor, a pause before speaking.

A scene opens without my permission.

A high wall. A doorway. Light spilling out.

I'm inside it as if I've always been approaching it.

I don't call it truth. I only note its presence.

I picture a centre held inside a six-fold shape.

A place that doesn't move.

Something in me longs to sit there and stop turning everything into a story.

The longing doesn't grant access. It only shows itself.

The image widens into colour and form—

bands, shapes, watchful edges—like a mind making architecture out of pressure.

I feel surrounded: half held, half threatened.

I don't interpret it. I let it pass through as weather.

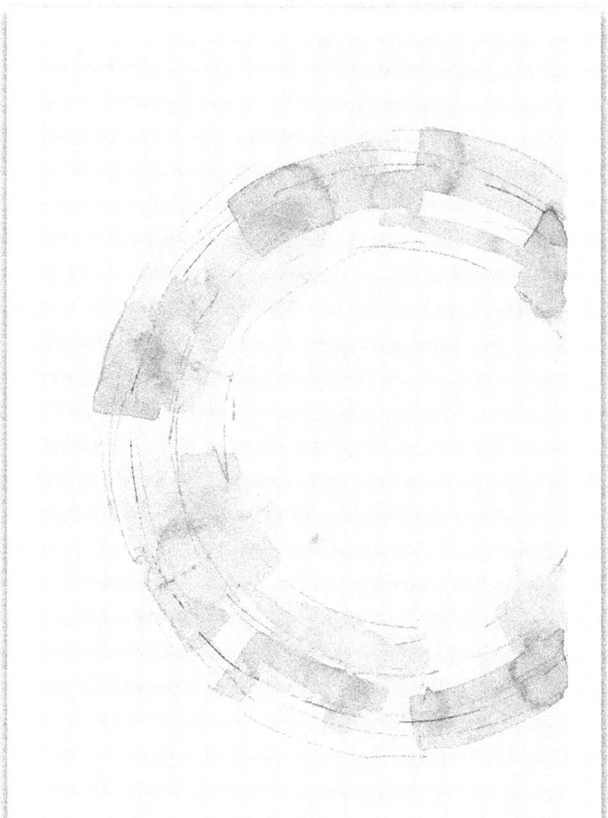

I'm spoken to like someone worth speaking to.

The voice doesn't erase my shame.

It doesn't agree with it either.

It stands beside me at the threshold and stays.